Mirabilis

Mirabilis

Poems by

Laura Ingram

Cover design by Shay Culligan

ISBN: 978-1-952326-10-3

Kelsay Books
502 South 1040 East, A-119
American Fork, Utah, 84003

In loving memory of Paige Gong

Acknowledgments

"Elsyium" Published with *Bone and Ink Magazine* Spring 2019

"After You Killed Yourself" Published with *Voice of Eve*
Fall Issue 2018

A Response to the Internet Article "5 Reasons to Date a Girl with
an Eating Disorder"—Published with *Forest for the Trees*
inaugural print issue, Spring 2016 and with Tilde Press Summer
2018

"Debunking the Butterfly Effect" Published winter 2017 with
Eunoia Review

"Visiting the Doll Hospital" Published Summer 2019 with
Voice of Eve

"Radical Notions" Published Spring 2015 with *Gravel Magazine*

"0: No Pain, Feeling Perfectly Normal" Published Winter 2019
with *Random Sample Review,* Nominated for Best of the
Net Fall 2019

Contents

Elysium

The one with the delicate ankles, whom Hadês[1] seized.

I eat my dreams with a knife and fork
chopped into bite-sized pieces
all six of Persephone's swallows
dark juice dribbling down.

Death comes to me, again,
pressing her chapped mouth to the door
until she leaves a wet ring in the wood
mauve arms encircling me like Dawes Gap
dim of night following her in on all fours
like the lumber of a soft black dog.

It's not as terrible as you've been told,
she says, taking my cheeks in two hands,
rings scraping the skin
pale as the blood of butterflies—
her grip so tight she nearly cracks my mandible
eyes leaking out like egg yolks.

Morning scratches its yellow back against the windows again,
cupboards bare
paring knife sud-soaked in the sink
my hunger simpler than soft soap
The whispered lecture of the wall clock
teaching me not to want.

After You Killed Yourself

A flat-fronted school bus skids into a snow bank
Singe file third-graders pinging out everywhere like a
snapped string of seed pearls.

Only your last name made the news. No high school head shot.
My unmade bed is the mortician's tilted table
half-sleep the scalpel to my sternum
dreams yanking my heart out, hand over hand.

I wake with the sweaty sheet pulled up to my eyes.

Mornings stay slick, embalmed by splashes of instant coffee
I use your shampoo in the shower
remember reading that hair keeps growing for a week or two after.
I step out of the spray
snip my ponytail just below the chin.

I cannot see my face in the mirror fog—
only the shrugging of shoulders—
the dark damp of my hair clogging the drain.
I drive, city slum scratching its back against my car windows
sky static as the jazz station.

I park farther away from the Walgreens than I need to
still at the front window's Tylenol tower.
Touching my fingertips to my unmoved mouth in the glass,
I startle at my own chapped lips
skinny legs and split ends
coffee stain on my coat pocket.
I want to hug myself so incipient—

pressing a chaste kiss to the distillery
of a window reflection, mauves muted
I go in to buy my toothbrush.
I remember you.

0: No pain. Feeling Perfectly Normal.

The invention of zero has, at the very least, two supposed points of discovery. Absolute zero, the temperature at which molecules stop bumping shoulders, is negative 273 degrees colder than the freezing point of water. Zero resides among numbers, between their measured, often insignificant infinities, but zero does not behave as a number must. Zero, indivisible as an atom, arose, as religion arises, shrouded in mythos and, for the most part, unproven.

Zero, in Tennis, is said by some to be a misinterpretation, of course by Americans, of the French world 'l'oeuf", or "the egg", referring to the shape zero takes at its almost tangible. Others argue that zero in Tennis is love, with only love of the sport keeping scoreless players on the court. Zero, the dress size, is anywhere from an inch and a half to half an inch larger than double-zero. Triple-zero, across the few major retailers that carry it, runs the same as double zero.

Watching my pants pool at the ankle, I divide myself by the space left over when I sit on a bus seat. I am nothing.

The answer is undefined.

Amongst Other Things

me, shuffling round the lavender dim of the kitchen
like the planchette on a Ouija board ,
palms two scraps of crepe-de-chine,
albino hurricane rapping her split knuckles against the window
squinting the sty from her eye.

me, gracelessly kicking the car door closed
against the cold,
chapped face pinker than Poland,
clutching the paper bag rattling with your prescriptions,
bottles pale as the blood of butterflies
with both hands.

A Response to the Return of King's article "5 reasons to date a girl with an eating disorder."

5. She is better in bed.

She sterilizes herself with Chanel No. 5. Her clavicles bud with bluebells at the brush of your fingers.

In the time of tuberculosis, when a man wanted to impress a woman, he would learn the language of flowers.

Most of the perennials were meant for apologies.

She insists you scrub the dirt from beneath your nail beds before she slides under the sheet. You didn't know love was something with prerequisites.

She doesn't have to know you only kiss her pelvic bones for practice. She won't remember the alias for alarm you whisper in her ear.

When surgical students are training with cadavers, the fat comes off before they open up.

She will love you and love you until she is empty, behind closed doors and beneath open palms again.

4. Probably has money of her own

She picks up the tab when you take her out for sushi, tap the tines of her fork against her teacup, cleaves her lettuce into crescents while your friends stare, and when she gets up to go to the bathroom, they ask you what is wrong with her and you pretend not to know.

She comes back to the table, eyes red and whirring as the evening news, leaves a generous tip.

When you lean down to kiss her goodnight, her mouth has been replaced with a hotline number.

3. She is fragile and vulnerable.

       Her doctors worry she will fall and break her hip. She worries you will remember she is only ulna and aspartame, and leave her in search of something more solid.

       She never leaves dishes in the sink, but her hair is falling out, and her sweater isn't clean.

2. She will probably cost less money

       Her nightmares are the color of magazines. She trims diet plans out of Women's Day in hospital waiting rooms, laminates her frontal lobe, cancels her subscription to the cerebellum. You watch her rustle into a backless paper gown, wonder if, as a little girl, she ever sliced supermodels from the pages of her sister's seventeen, snipped off bits of their legs and creased them into chair's at Barbie's kitchen table.

       You take her to a dietitian, a psychiatrist, a holistic healer. The bills grapple with her pill bottles for space on the countertop.

       She apologizes when men with small eyes and large hands tell you she is dying; they do not.

1. Her Obsession with Her Body will Improve her Overall Appearance

       She knows the reflection she flushes down the toilet is distorted, but she looks smaller here than in any of the mirrors.

       She stares at herself in the flat side of the spoons when she rinses the silverware, organizes the knives dull-side down, but you still worry that she will hurt herself with a salad fork.

       She never leaves the house without makeup, always rinses her mouth before cringing from your kiss.

       Date a girl with an eating disorder. Watch her ghost from the body in your bed to a body in a box.

       All that's left is a life of hospital corners and cereal getting soggy.

       Both of you on your knees.

Psalm to Tinker Creek

Shushed between aspen and spruce,
body crouched as cursive
                    by the creek bed
I am awed
by the swarming of hours,
        the sneakers of sophomore students
        trampling asphalt flowers,
        voices shrilling across the dusk
        While I, jostled as birth
        mud caked beneath my nail beds

        misremember the deer my father hit
        Driving home in the October pink
        from piano class—
headlights gleaming like mardi-gras beads
        the urge to snap my own ankles
        cease in that same immaculate curl,
cover my broken bones with dark earth—
        quiet as ancient fern's stay kept.

Radical Notions

At the low end of eleven, I have shiny shoes and shiny hair. I have six pairs of lace edged socks and two pink training bras. Boys snap the bands on the back when I bend over at the water fountain.

I do not tell the teacher. She will tell me they are mean because they like me.

I do not know how to use the can opener. I do not know why my mother is crying behind closed doors. I do not know where I will be going to middle school. I do not know when I will stop being scared of what my grandmother calls "becoming a woman." I do not know if I will ever figure out what this means and why people always whisper behind their hands about it, going back and forth like fans, futile at cooling the coming pressure system.

I am not supposed to shut the door because I share a room with my sister, but sometimes I do when she is out on someone else's stoop, with a boy whose mouth is like Moscow in mid November, knocking her teeth together, leaving pedestrians chilled.

When he puts his hands on her, she shivers down like snow.

If he put his hands on me, I would cut them off.

***

The boys in my class make fun of my best friend because she is afraid. They make fun of me because I am not. I punch Austin Miller and get sent to the principal. Nobody seems to appreciate the knuckle blood but me.

I stop skipping rope and start skipping breakfast. With closed fists and an open face, I count the swirls on my ceiling. Half past twelve, all the tremors and ticking do little to tell me what this time is supposed to be.

There are mosquito bites on my ankles, razor knicks on my heart.

My mother always warned me about things growing back thicker.

I, like every girl, worry while I wait.

Gloam

I am a long-boned eleven,
Listless as August fog,
eyes two snowdrop bulbs
sunken white like the sky inside my skull,
watching summer erupt from the sore earth
like new molars—

my mother saves all my baby teeth
in a broken eau de toilette bottle
brown as time
tucked beneath her nylons.
I snatch them from her bureau drawer
use six to mark the grave of a dead canary
the cat killed
scatter the rest into the rosebush.

Before setting the table with grandmother's chipped china,
she pulled her heart out from its box under the bed
crushed it with the sole
of one of my father's worn-out work-boots
both of us crying in our dimming bedrooms
with the doors closed.

Debunking the Butterfly Effect

One
Born between entropy and atrophy, I scream as if I have every right to.

Two
Still jaundiced as the dawn's blistered palm, my first phase references the mediocrity of myth, crescent teeth waning gibbous tongue; I tell my mother the man in the moon knows my middle name.

Three
Omniscient as God, I bounce around the baby seat on the back of my mother's bike. Our street would fit in the top shelf of a China Cabinet.

Four
I twirl around my room, steps asymmetrical as an analog signal, fingers curled into fists like the magnetic tape inside of cassettes.

Five
The teacher makes me student of the week more than once but I don't like to lead the line.

Six
I perform an appendectomy on Barbie, one of her pink plastic pumps serving as the scalpel, barricade the decapitated Ken doll from the Dream House door with tiny teal cups from the set my sister never wanted.

Seven

I have six pairs of lace-trimmed socks and two cherry alligator clips, as well as the worst handwriting in the class. I staple seven sheets of coral construction paper, come to my mother clutching at the color. I have taken it upon myself to recount the birth of a bird in cloud-spat blue block letters. No one except the wind had such irascible wrists.

Eight

I get my first library card, dry dandelions between the page breaks. I hope to grow my hair down to my hipbones or heels, to go to bed hungry like the gilded girls flitting through a thousand forests in perfect asymmetry.

Nine

The school nurse passes a maxi pad, pink as Poland, around the room, tells us we were born with all the eggs we'd ever need to make babies already in our ovaries. Watching myself wince in the space between the mirror and me, I decide something as brutal as girlhood isn't meant to be discrete.

Ten

My rapid eye movement follows the Fibonacci sequence; I dream between catechism and chasm. My friend and I cover the grave of another class's guinea pig with pine needles during recess, cry as if we have every right to.

Eleven

I teach myself elementary Latin and intermediate American Sign Language, shiver through another lesson in almost. I coerce myself into a crush on a boy with eyes like Orion, although his mouth may be the biggest impact crater on this side of ephemera, and despite him thinking Anna McPherson is prettier and telling me so.
So much of our love is convinced.

Twelve

I speak softer than the Seine, shuffle the heels of my hands, skid through the hallways in silver Mary Janes, shudder in a beige bathroom stall for the first fifteen minutes of Friday afternoon gym, cradle my skull between both forefingers and thumbs, act as the archaeologist of my own anonymity.

Thirteen

The boy behind me in English class calls me Auschwitz after we discuss the diary of Anne Frank, insists the department stores don't make skinny jeans skinny enough for me. The half-life of anorexia is always; I shiver between oxidation numbers, metacarpals one electron reduction below destabilization.

Fourteen

Seventy-six pounds of gossamer and syncope, I show up for my first day at the local arts high school in a checkered skirt from the children's department, enchant my classmates with my squeaky voice and squeaky shoes.

Fifteen

Gawky and static as a grade school graduation, no one points but everyone stares at my clavicle breaking into blossom like a lilac or the long green hair of a headstone from my rotting body.

Sixteen

The smaller that I get, the larger the slouching city where I sleep seems, its decaffeinated expressways brighter and emptier than me. I spend six months in the hospital, grow as if I have every right to.

Seventeen

My class crowns me homecoming queen, but someone has to show me where I stand;
I'm not sure who I am when my hands have stopped shaking.

Eighteen

I swallow my shimmering dreams, wake as if I have every right to.

Morning Song

Dawn shrills from the beak of a goldfinch
pink and chapped as a kiss to the temple
dreams scaling down
from the second story window ,
scampering off on all fours.

I wake up
sun under my tongue,
pour my pulse into a chipped coffee mug,
gulp.

Visiting the Doll Hospital

Christ has his second coming
as my Granddad's coat
 with me, clattering after him like a coin tossed
atop a card table
December sun squinting its unlashed eye and
President Hoover's promises
interrupting the piano's chattering teeth
false contralto ringing from the radio by the cash register.

Me, cupping the chipped china cheek of my Shirley temple doll,
her pink glass lips
blunt and glimmering as a bad dream,
her broken arm tied to her chest with cheesecloth.
My Sunday school shoes fib to the Persian rug

Heaven is a place downtown two blocks from the Bay
porcelain limbs stacked to the ceiling

Startling somewhere between linen and lace
at shelf after shelf of cephalophores in silk
only half having hats
to cover their hearts.

No one has ever taught me to pray—
at least, not completely
but I fall down
idle and mouthing
holy as glass
blessing boxes of broken alabaster bodies
as if they, like me
were daughters
thread hanging from
their handmade hearts.

Je Voudrais

Velvet ribbon round my neck,
clavicle scrawled against my skin like a pharmacist's signature;
Chantilly and chiffon chattering to each other in a whitewood
wardrobe.
The lavender dim of a Stuttgart studio;
to never startle at my own sternum
in the gilded mirror again.

Hair dark as famine hanging to my hipbones
Saint Catherine to have her second coming
as my tattered satin coat,
her pink shimmer buttoned around my ribs
while I bow my head between
hypoglycemia and hypocrisy
before Sunday lunch
elbows ruffling the lace tablecloth,
pray to every name in the new testament
that I will not want.

To anoint myself with Chanel Number 5
genuflect before a teetering bookcase
teeming with annotated editions;
Plath and Pound.

Two chipped china mugs and
enough quarters for phone calls home
from a foreign city's American noise.
For the snow to never soak
through the soles of my shoes again.

About the Author

Laura Ingram is a tiny girl with big glasses and bigger ideas. Her poetry and prose have been published in over seventy literary journals, among them *The Cactus Heart Review, Gravel, Glass Kite Anthology* and *Voice of Eve.* Her first collection, *Junior Citizen's Discount,* was released with Desert Willow Press May 2018; her children's book *Stand Up* Was subsequently released with Nesting Tree books August 2018. Laura loves Harry Potter and Harry Styles. She is a sophomore creative writing student.

Made in the USA
Middletown, DE
27 September 2024

61596523R00021